D1546562

DAN MARINO
A LOOK BACK AT A LEGEND

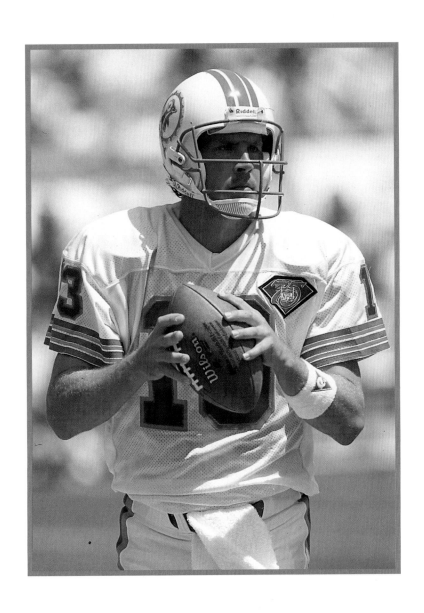

DOLPHIN/CURTIS PUBLISHING
MIAMI, FLORIDA

Acknowledgements

Dan Marino supplied NFL fans with 17 seasons of great football memories. *Dolphin Digest* has covered every game of his spectacular career. The entire staff of writers, editors and photographers, past and present, have made this book possible.

This project would never have reached completion without the invaluable help and cooperation of many, including the Miami Dolphins. Thanks to records and archives director Kristin Hingston for her assistance and patience; Scott Stone and Rodney Wood of the publications department for filling in the many blanks; and team photographer Dave Cross for his talent and expertise.

A special thank you to the Dan Marino Foundation for their support and the wonderful work they do for the children of South Florida.

DAN MARINO
A LOOK BACK AT A LEGEND

Editor, Coordinator
Ken Keidel

Creative Director
Armando Mato

Research/Editing
Alain Poupart

Copy Research
Bill Daley

TABLE OF CONTENTS

FOREWORD

As I look back on my 17 seasons with the Miami Dolphins, there are so many great memories. From my rookie year when everything just seemed to fall in place, to the record-breaking season of 1984, and on through the years, it was an honor to be part of the Miami Dolphins' winning tradition.

I feel fortunate to have played my entire career with the same team, and to have enjoyed so much success. My coaches and teammates deserve much of the credit. Without people like Don Shula, Don Strock, Nat Moore, Mark Clayton, Mark Duper, Dwight Stephenson, Jim Jensen, O.J. McDuffie and so many others, none of the things I accomplished would have been possible.

There is another teammate I would like to thank — and that is you, the fan. I believe the Miami Dolphins have the best fans in the NFL. We shared some wonderful moments and I will always be thankful for those great memories.

I hope this book allows you to relive many of those moments. It is an outstanding collection of photographs from my career with the Dolphins. Enjoy and, again, thanks for your support through the years.

Dan Marino
13

Dan Marino reported to camp as the Miami Dolphins' No. I selection in the 1983 draft. Seventeen seasons later, he would retire from the only team he ever played for, holding virtually every major NFL passing record.

Don Shula (r) introduces Marino to Dolphins owner Joe Robbie during his first day at training camp.

Shula then introduces Marino to the fans at the Dolphins kickoff banquet in May of 1983.

1983

ROOKIE YEAR

Marino brought many talents to the field, but no one could imagine the career that lie ahead for the young rookie.

'83 NUMBERS

Games: 11
Starts: 9
Attempts: 296
Completions: 173
Yards: 2210
Completion pct.: 58.4
Touchdowns: 20
Interceptions: 6
Team record: 12-4

Oct. 9, 1983: In his first start Marino throws for 322 yards and three touchdowns in an overtime loss to Buffalo.

Coach Don Shula quickly adjusted his game strategies to the talents of his emerging young quarterback.

Nov. 6, 1983: With a 20-17 win in San Francisco, Marino had led the Dolphins to four straight wins, three on the road.

FAST *fact*

Despite playing the equivalent of only 10 games in 1983, Marino became the first rookie quarterback chosen to start in the Pro Bowl, and was the first rookie quarterback to lead a conference in passer rating (96.0) since the AFL-NFL merger in 1970.

13

Dan Marino entered his second season as a rising star, confident and fully in charge of the offense.

Sept. 2, 1984: Marino and Shula scout the opening-day foe, the Washington Redskins, prior to kickoff.

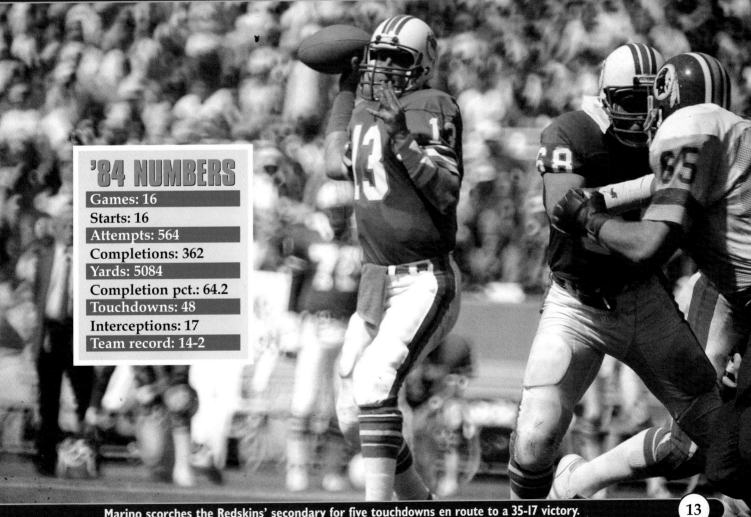

'84 NUMBERS

Games: 16
Starts: 16
Attempts: 564
Completions: 362
Yards: 5084
Completion pct.: 64.2
Touchdowns: 48
Interceptions: 17
Team record: 14-2

Marino scorches the Redskins' secondary for five touchdowns en route to a 35-17 victory.

FAST *fact*

Marino led the Dolphins to an 11-0 start in 1984, the team's best since the undefeated 1972 season.

Dec. 29, 1984: Marino tosses three TDs against Seattle and gets the first playoff win of his career.

SUPER XIX BOWL

Jan. 20, 1985: Marino and the Dolphins head into the Super Bowl with a 16-2 record and high hopes for the team's third Lombardi Trophy.

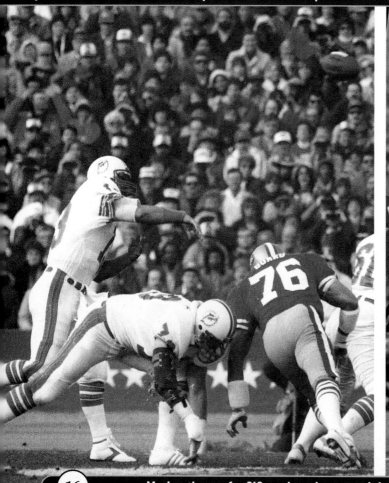

Marino throws for 318 yards and one touchdown to Dan Johnson (above), but the 49ers prevail 38-16.

> It's real nice and exciting for me to break the records, but it's more exciting for me to be on a winning team.

Marino's 48 TD passes in '84 were more than 24 of Miami's 25 other QBs threw in their entire Dolphins careers.

1984: A RECORD YEAR

Dan Marino set seven NFL records, including five which still stood at the end of the 1999 season, and tied one other during what was the greatest year ever for an NFL quarterback.

RECORDS BROKEN

- Most passing yards: 5,084
- Most games, 400 or more yards passing: 4
- Most touchdown passes: 48
- Most completions: 362 (broken by Houston's Warren Moon in 1991)
- Most games, four or more touchdown passes: 6
- Most consecutive games, four or more touchdown passes: 4
- Most games, 300 or more yards passing: 9 (tied by Houston's Warren Moon in 1990 and St. Louis' Kurt Warner in 1999)

RECORD TIED

- Most consecutive games, 400 or more yards passing: 2 (Dan Fouts, San Diego, 1982; Phil Simms, N.Y. Giants, 1985)

Thanks Dan,
for 17 years of excitement,
and for appearing on the cover
of Dolphin Digest 73 times

From the Staff of Dolphin Digest

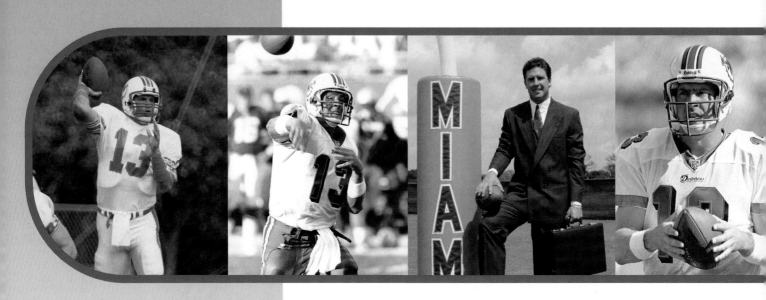

For subscription information call:
1-800-334-4005
or check us out on the web:
dolphindigest.com

Marino's 5,084 passing yards in '84 is the only 5,000-yard season in NFL history.

19

FAST *fact*

Marino needed only eight games in 1984 to break Bob Griese's team record for touchdown passes in a season (22).

◆◆◆

Despite being in only his second season, he was named in a 1984 CBS poll and in the *New York Times* as the most popular player in pro football.

Coming off a Super Bowl appearance in 1984, Marino was looking for big things as the '85 season opened.

Sept. 22, 1985: Marino throws two TDs and the Dolphins' defense takes control in a 31-0 shutout of the Chiefs.

Dec. 22, 1985: Marino and the Dolphins tune up for the playoffs with a 28-0 blanking of Buffalo in the regular season finale.

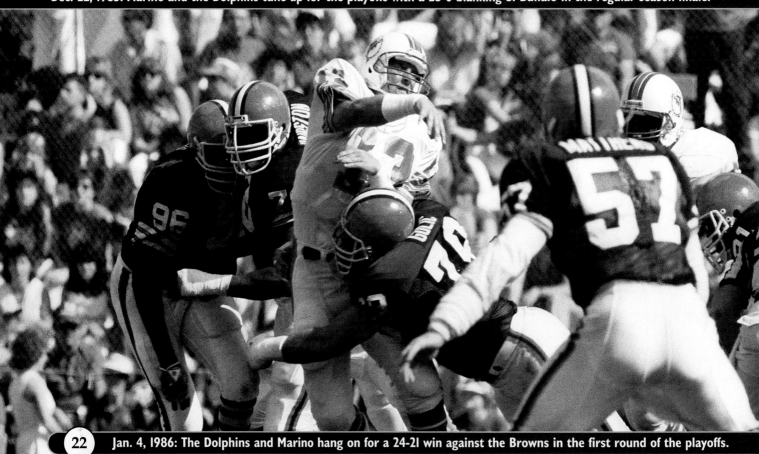

Jan. 4, 1986: The Dolphins and Marino hang on for a 24-21 win against the Browns in the first round of the playoffs.

Marino led the NFL in yards (4,137), completions (336) and touchdowns (30) in 1985.

There would be no return to the Super Bowl in '85 as Miami fell to New England 31-14 in the AFC Championship Game.

1986
4th SEASON

24 The Dolphins lost four of their first five games in '86, including a loss to the 49ers that saw Marino throw four interceptions.

Sept. 2I, I986: Marino throws a team-record six touchdowns in a heartbreaking 5I-45 OT loss to the Jets.

'86 NUMBERS

Games: 16
Starts: 16
Attempts: 623
Completions: 378
Yards: 4746
Completion pct.: 60.7
Touchdowns: 44
Interceptions: 23
Team record: 8-8

The 1986 season would be the Dolphins' last at the Orange Bowl and the first where Marino would not be in the playoffs.

Dec. 14, 1986: Coach Shula, Don Strock and Marino plan strategy before the start of overtime against the Rams.

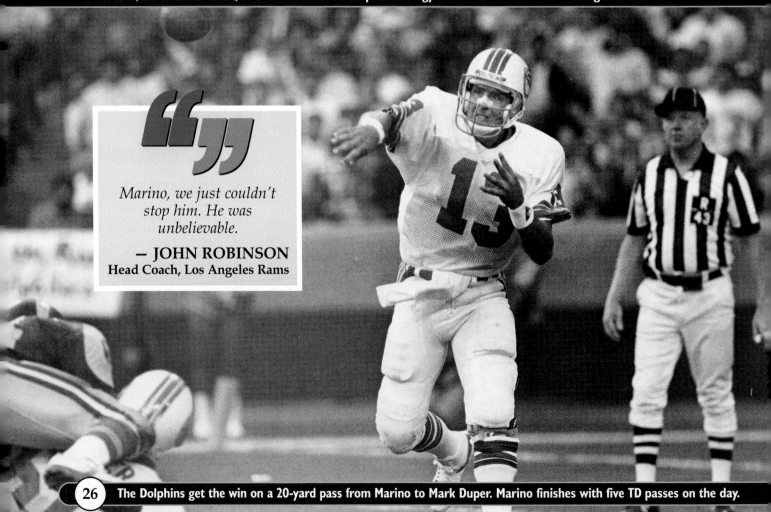

Marino, we just couldn't stop him. He was unbelievable.

— JOHN ROBINSON
Head Coach, Los Angeles Rams

The Dolphins get the win on a 20-yard pass from Marino to Mark Duper. Marino finishes with five TD passes on the day.

1987

STRIKE SEASON

MUSICIANS
OF THE
PHIL.HAR...
♪ SUPP...
N.F...
PLA...
AS...

HARMONIC
MUSICIANS,
EMBERS OF
CAL 655 A.F. of M
SUPPORT
MIAMI DOLPHINS
ND THE NFLPA

NATIONAL FOOTBALL LEAGUE

PLAYERS

ON STRIKE

- For Fair
  Player Contracts

- For Better Pension
  For All Players,
  1920 Through 1990

The 1987 season was interrupted by a players strike, a cause Dan Marino believed in, and other local unions supported.

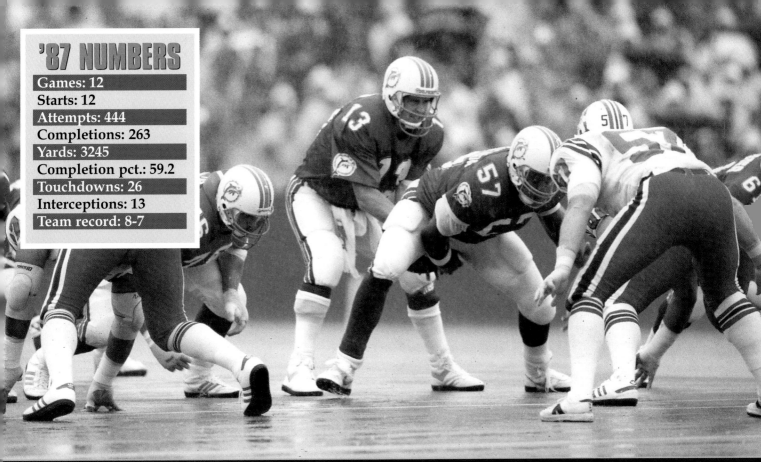

'87 NUMBERS

Games: 12
Starts: 12
Attempts: 444
Completions: 263
Yards: 3245
Completion pct.: 59.2
Touchdowns: 26
Interceptions: 13
Team record: 8-7

Sept. 13, 1987: The season starts with a soggy loss at New England. Two weeks later, NFL players go on strike for a month.

Oct. 25, 1987: When the season resumes, Marino throws four TDs but the Dolphins fall to the Bills in overtime.

Nov. 8, 1987: Marino and Bengals QB Boomer Esiason before their matchup in Cincinnati.

Esiason ended the season leading the AFC in passing yardage, with Marino second, but the Dolphins quarterback came out on top this day as Miami won 20-14.

FAST fact

A string of 50 consecutive starts came to an end in 1987 when Marino did not play in the three replacement games during the strike.

1988 would be Dan Marino's only losing season as the Dolphins dropped six of the last seven games to finish 6-10.

'88 NUMBERS

Games: 16
Starts: 16
Attempts: 606
Completions: 354
Yards: 4434
Completion pct.: 58.4
Touchdowns: 28
Interceptions: 23
Team record: 6-10

Sept. 18, 1988: Marino throws touchdowns to Mark Clayton and Ferrell Edmunds in the home opener, a 24-17 win over the Packers.

In 1988 Marino led the NFL in attempts (606), completions (354), and yards (4,434).

Oct. 30, 1988: Marino and the Dolphins beat the Buccaneers in one of only two road wins during the season.

"
You can throw for 900 yards, but if you throw an interception at a time when you've got a chance to tie the game, the statistics don't matter.

— DAN MARINO

Oct. 23, 1988: Marino throws 60 times for a team-record 521 yards in a home loss to the Jets.

35

Autographed Collector's Prints

"Marino to Clayton - Records Fall"   15" x 18"

Quarterback Dan Marino has announced his retirement and moved a step closer to the Hall of Fame. Dan broke virtually every passing record imaginable as he established himself as one of the greatest football players of all time. Dan's number one receiver over his career was the perennial all-pro Mark Clayton. Dan and Mark found the end zone an amazing 79 times.

Cindy Erkfitz-Sirls, one of the world's most renowned sports artists has captured this in her art work entitled "Marino to Clayton - Records Fall". A very limited edition of only 959 lithograph prints has been produced, each print has been personally autographed by Marino and Clayton, then signed and numbered by the artist and are available at the cost of $460.00 each (price includes shipping and handling). The lithographs have been authenticated by using the Upper Deck

holographic seal to protect the integrity and to guarantee the authenticity of Upper Deck Authenticated products and signatures. A numbered hologram seal on the product and matching number on the certificate of ownership identify and verify each item.

Sure to be a collector's item with only 959 prints being released, this should be a great investment as well as a work of art to be treasured by football fans. This is a rare and valuable opportunity to own what we believe is the only limited edition artwork to contain <u>both</u> of these stars autographs. You'll receive your print within 2 to 5 working days from the time your order is received. If you are not 100% satisfied, you have 30 days to return the print for a full refund. To place an order or to find out more about Cindy's art, just call her at the toll free number listed on this order form.

Send Check or Money Order to: Cindy Erkfitz-Sirls • 810 ENCANTO ST. • CORONA, CA 92881

CREDIT CARD ORDERS CALL TOLL FREE: 1-800-444-4278

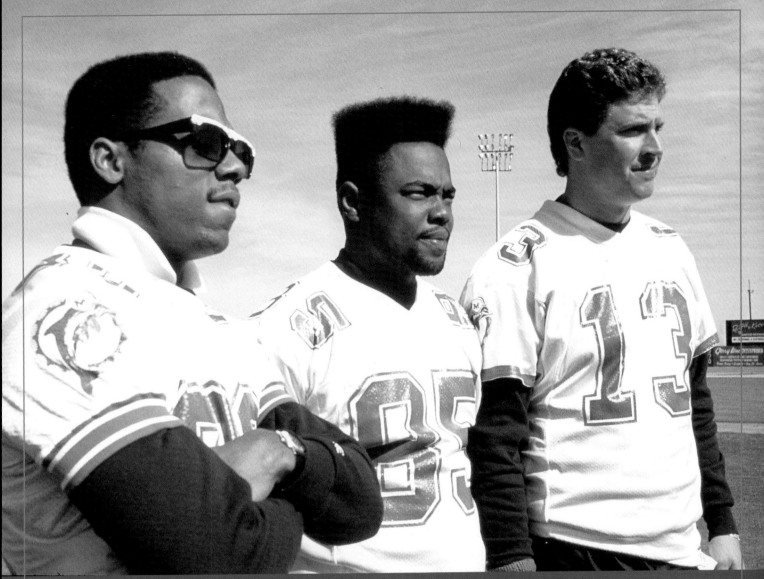

Mark Clayton (l.) and Mark Duper (c.) were on the receiving end of Marino passes for a combined total of 16,943 yards.

If Dan didn't like a play they'd send in, he'd say. '(Bleep) that play.' Then he'd say, 'OK. Duper. Clayton. Get open. I'll get it to you.' That's what we'd do. We'd go out and haul downfield. And he'd get it to us.

— WR MARK DUPER

FAST *fact*

A total of 80 different receivers caught passes from Marino during his career — including Marino, who caught a deflected pass on a play that wound up losing 6 yards against New England in 1995.

38 Sept. 17, 1989: Marino throws his 200th career touchdown pass, a 10-yarder to Jim Jensen in a 24-10 win at New England.

'89 NUMBERS

Games: 16
Starts: 16
Attempts: 550
Completions: 308
Yards: 3997
Completion pct.: 56.0
Touchdowns: 24
Interceptions: 22
Team record: 8-8

The Dolphins'
NFL-record streak of
19 consecutive games
without a sack allowed
comes to an end
against Buffalo on
Oct. 29, 1989

Bruce Smith and the Bills make it a rough day for Marino and the Dolphins, a 31-17 loss.

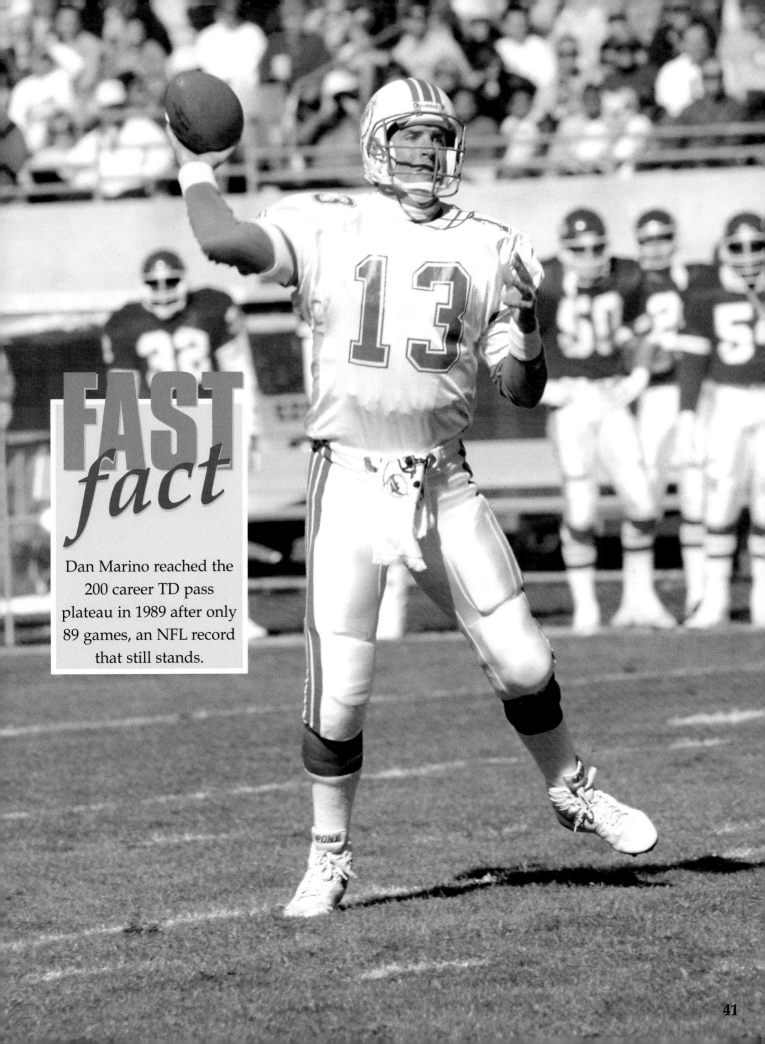

FAST *fact*

Dan Marino reached the 200 career TD pass plateau in 1989 after only 89 games, an NFL record that still stands.

Dan Marino was all business when he posed for this Dolphin Digest cover in July of 1990.

In 1990 Marino reached 30,000 career yards in his 114th game, faster than any other QB in NFL history.

> *That fire, it was in Marino's eyes. I could tell right then that we were going to score.*
>
> **— WR JIM JENSEN**
> on Miami's last-second drive to beat the Jets

Oct. 7, 1990: Marino throws a 69-yard TD to Mark Duper against the Jets as the Dolphins record the second of six consecutive victories.

> " "
>
> *I thought 34 points would be enough to win this game. But the Bills didn't make too many mistakes.*
>
> **— DAN MARINO**

1991
9th SEASON

Aug. 4, 1991: Future Hall of Famers Howie Long (inducted in July 2000) and Dan Marino before the American Bowl in Tokyo.

Nov. 10, 1991: Marino enjoys a postgame press conference after throwing three touchdowns in a 30-20 win vs. New England.

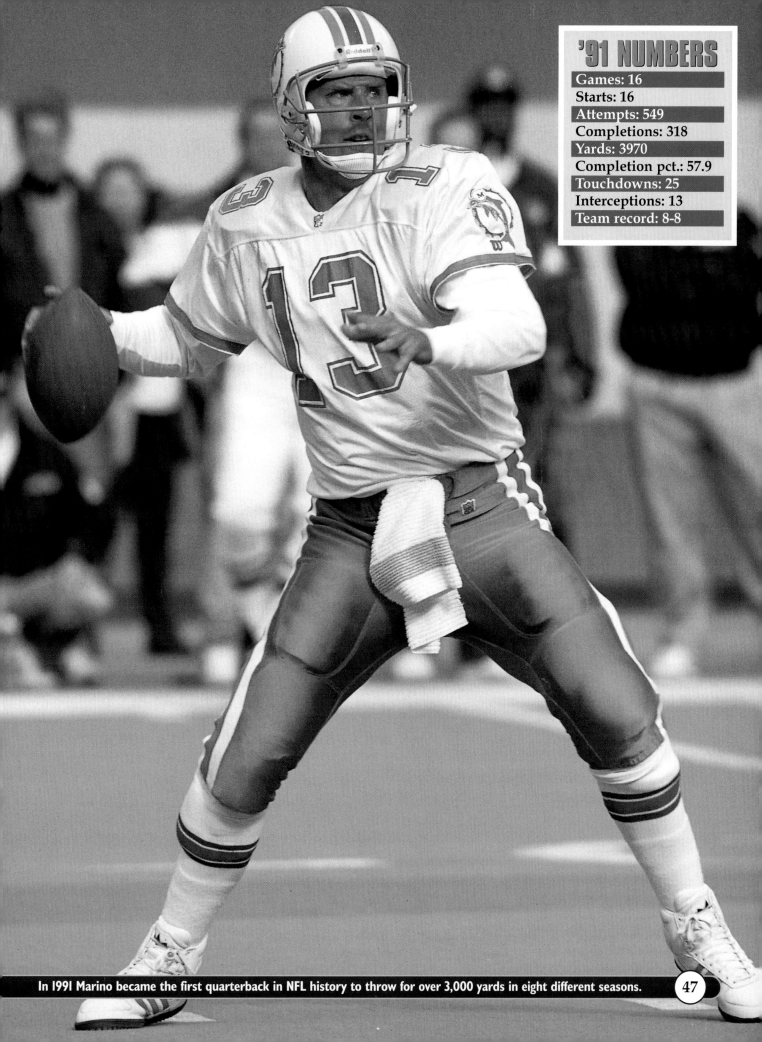

In 1991 Marino became the first quarterback in NFL history to throw for over 3,000 yards in eight different seasons.

Dec. 15, 1991: Marino throws for three touchdowns and runs for another, but the Dolphins fall to the Chargers 38-30.

> *It seems like every week, Danny is breaking another record. It's hard to keep track of all of them.*
>
> **— GUARD KEITH SIMS**

After three years without being named to the Pro Bowl, Marino was selected in 1991 for the sixth time in his career.

49

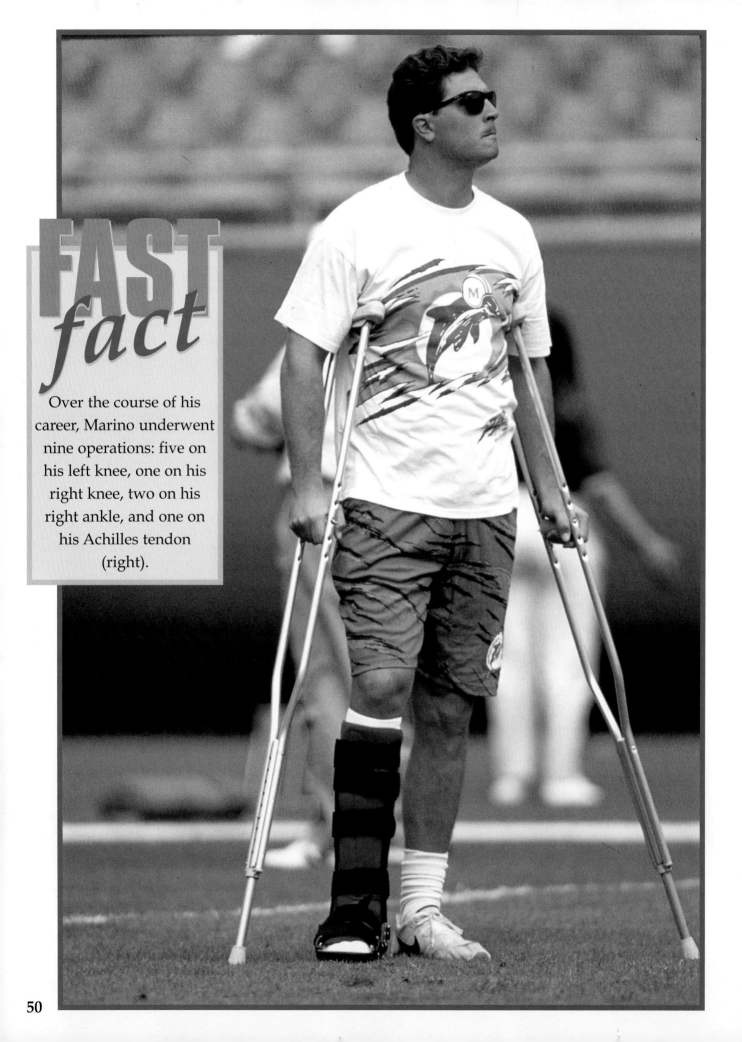

Over the course of his career, Marino underwent nine operations: five on his left knee, one on his right knee, two on his right ankle, and one on his Achilles tendon (right).

51

52 Aug. 16, 1992: Friends and future Hall of Fame quarterbacks Dan Marino and John Elway prior to the American Bowl in Berlin.

'92 NUMBERS

Games: 16
Starts: 16
Attempts: 554
Completions: 330
Yards: 4116
Completion pct.: 59.6
Touchdowns: 24
Interceptions: 16
Team record: 11-5

Marino and the Dolphins posted six straight victories to start the season, including a 37-10 win at Buffalo.

Dan Marino led the Dolphins to six fourth-quarter comebacks in 1992, his most ever in one season.

Jan. 10, 1993: Team owner Wayne Huizenga hugs Marino after his three-TD performance in a 31-0 playoff win over San Diego.

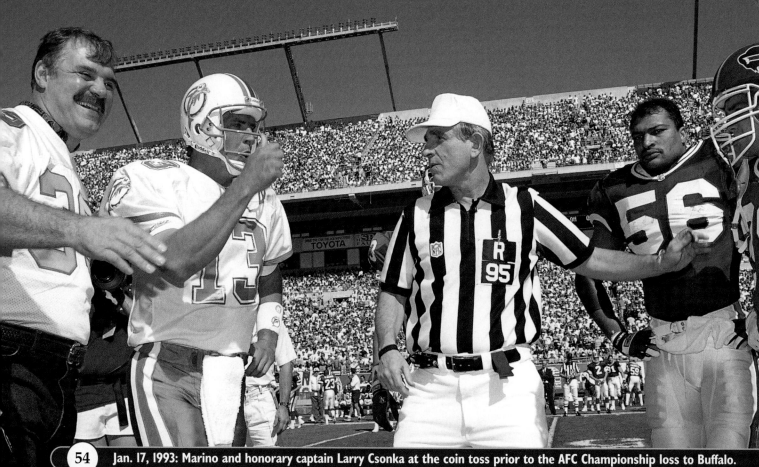

Jan. 17, 1993: Marino and honorary captain Larry Csonka at the coin toss prior to the AFC Championship loss to Buffalo.

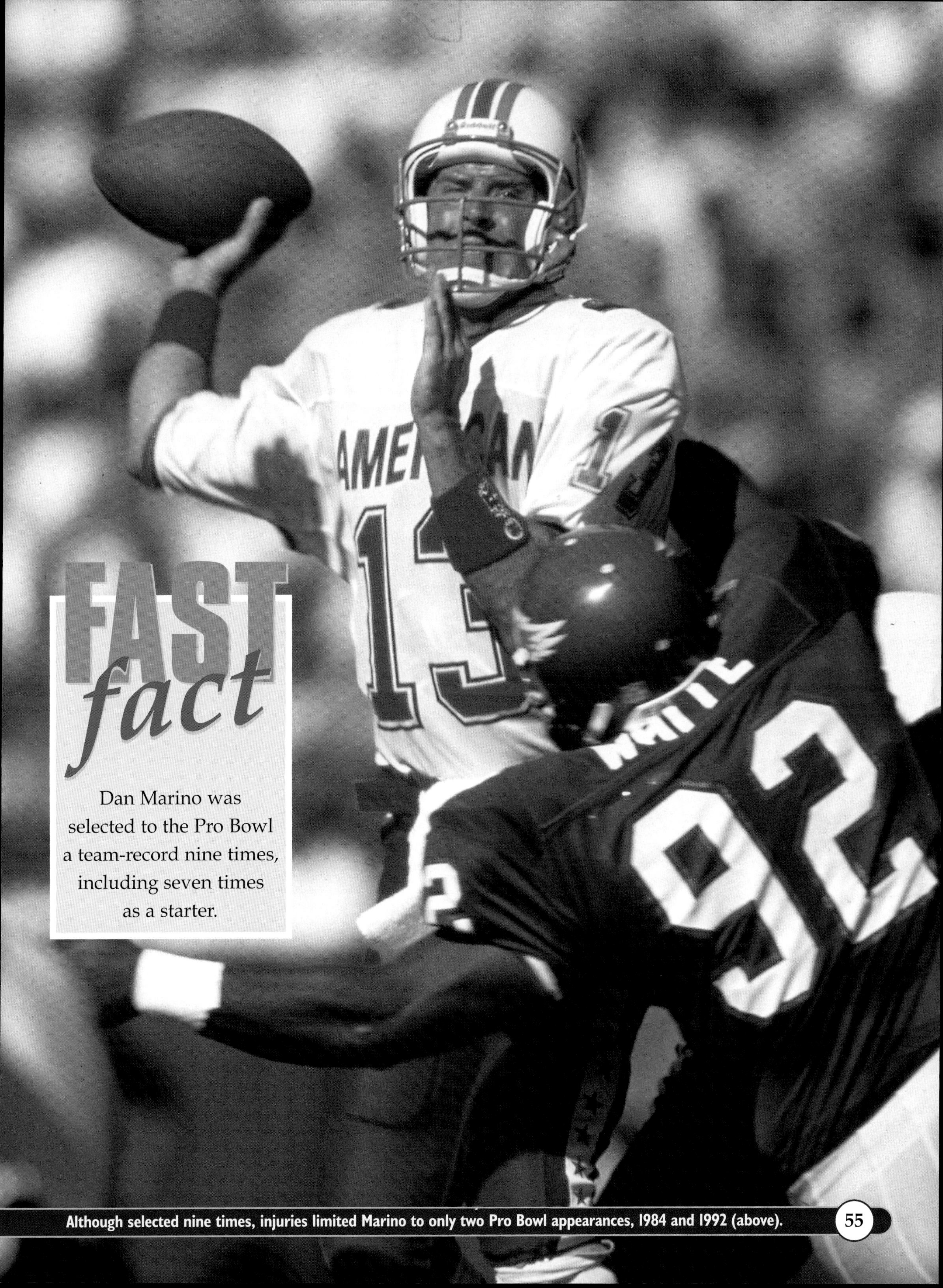

FAST
fact

Dan Marino was
selected to the Pro Bowl
a team-record nine times,
including seven times
as a starter.

Although selected nine times, injuries limited Marino to only two Pro Bowl appearances, 1984 and 1992 (above).

DAN MARINO'S NFL RECORDS

Most career passing attempts 8,358

Most career completions...4,967

Most career passing yards 61,361

Most career touchdown passes...420

Highest passer rating for a rookie ....96.0 in 1983

Highest completion percentage for a rookie
....58.45 in 1983 *(173 of 296)*

Most passing yards in a season.........................5,084 in 1984

Most career games with 400 or more yards passing 13

Most games in one season with 400 or more
yards passing...4 in 1984

Most career games with 300 or more yards passing 60

Most seasons with 3,000 or more
yards passing ....13 *(1984-92, 1994-95, 1997-98)*

Most consecutive seasons with 3,000 or more
yards passing ....9 *(1984-92)*

Most touchdown passes in a season.....................48 in 1984

Most career games with four of more
touchdown passes 21

Most games in a season with four or more
touchdown passes ....6 in 1984

Most consecutive games with four or more
touchdown passes ....4 in 1984

Lowest percentage of passes intercepted in
a rookie season ....2.03 in 1983 *(6 in 296 attempts)*

Most seasons leading the league in
passing attempts.....................5 *(1984, 1986, 1988, 1992, 1997)*

Most seasons leading the league in
completions..............................6 *(1984-86, 1988, 1992, 1997)*

Record Books

Most seasons with 40 or more touchdown passes 2 (1984, 1986)

Most seasons with 20 or more touchdown passes 13 (1983-92, 1994-95, 1998)

Most consecutive seasons with 20 or more touchdown passes 10 (1983-92)

Fewest amount of games needed to reach 100 career TD passes ....44 (Sept. 7, 1986 at San Diego)

Fewest amount of games needed to reach 200 career TD passes ....89 (Sept. 17, 1989 at New England)

Fewest amount of games needed to reach 300 career TD passes ....157 (Sept. 4, 1994 vs. New England)

RECORDS TIED FOR

Most seasons leading the league in passing yards 5 (1984-86, 1988, 1992)
tied with Sonny Jurgensen (Philadelphia, 1961-62; Washington, 1966-67, 1969)

Most consecutive seasons leading the league in completions 3 (1984-86)
tied with George Blanda (Houston, 1963-65)

Most consecutive games with 400 or more yards passing 2 (1984)
tied with Dan Fouts (San Diego, 1982) and Phil Simms (N.Y. Giants, 1985)

Most consecutive seasons with 4,000 or more yards passing 3 (1984-86)
tied with Dan Fouts (San Diego, 1979-81)

Most games in one season with 300 or more yards passing 9 (1984)
tied with Warren Moon (Houston, 1990) and Kurt Warner (St. Louis, 1999)

1993
THE INJURY

Oct. 10, 1993: The Dolphins were off to a 3-1 start when Marino suffered a season-ending Achilles tendon injury in Cleveland.

Sept. 26, 1993: Marino with good friend — and rival — Jim Kelly following Miami's 22-13 win in Buffalo.

Marino already had thrown for 161 yards against the Browns before tearing his Achilles tendon in the second quarter.

Scott Mitchell (l.) took over the reins at QB while Marino helped Don Shula and the Dolphins from the sidelines.

> *Looking at Dan Marino standing on the sidelines on crutches, I couldn't help but think back to all the games that Dan has won for us and how important he is to our football team.*
>
> **— DON SHULA**
> **After his 325th victory**

Nov. 14, 1993: Although he couldn't be on the field, Marino was happy for Shula when he registered career coaching win number 325 in Philadelphia, breaking the NFL record held by George Halas.

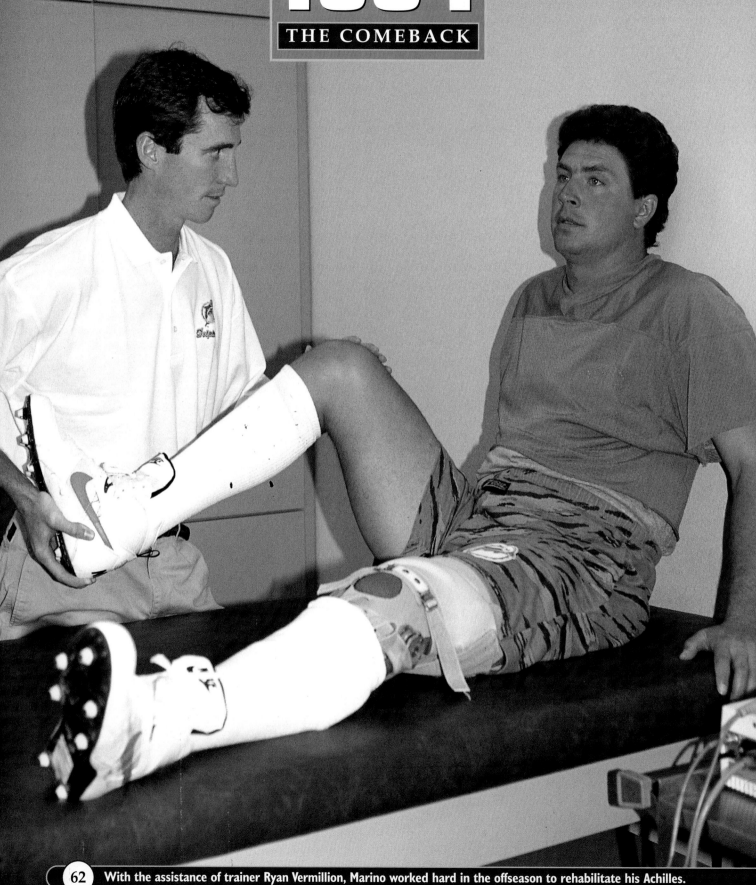

1994

THE COMEBACK

With the assistance of trainer Ryan Vermillion, Marino worked hard in the offseason to rehabilitate his Achilles.

'94 NUMBERS

Games: 16
Starts: 16
Attempts: 615
Completions: 385
Yards: 4453
Completion pct.: 62.6
Touchdowns: 30
Interceptions: 17
Team record: 10-6

Marino threw his 300th touchdown pass in 1994, joining Fran Tarkenton as the only quarterbacks to reach that milestone.

> ❝❞
>
> *What we witnessed today was one of the most phenomenal performances you'll ever see.*
>
> **— QB BERNIE KOSAR**
> **Following opening-day win over Patriots**

Sept. 4, 1994: There was little doubt Marino was back when he started the season with 473 yards and five touchdowns in a 39-35 win over New England.

> " " He is in such total control of things, it's hard to imagine anyone much better.
>
> — WR IRVING FRYAR

Marino led the Dolphins into the second round of the playoffs in '94, but Miami lost to San Diego 22-21 in the final moments.

1995
RECORDS FALL

Dan Marino broke NFL records for career attempts, completions and touchdown passes in 1995.

'95 NUMBERS

Games: 14
Starts: 14
Attempts: 482
Completions: 309
Yards: 3668
Completion pct.: 64.1
Touchdowns: 24
Interceptions: 15
Team record: 9-7

Sept. 3, 1995: Marino opens the season by throwing three TDs in a 52-14 thrashing of the Jets.

> "If my records had to be broken, I'm glad it's a class act like Danny who is breaking them.
>
> — FRAN TARKENTON

Oct. 8, 1995: Teammate Bryan Cox congratulates Marino after a 6-yard completion to Keith Byars against Indianapolis breaks Fran Tarkenton's NFL record for most career completions (3,687).

Nov. 26, 1995: Don Shula greets Marino after his 6-yard TD pass to Keith Byars helps him surpass Tarkenton's NFL record for career touchdown passes (343).

Dec. 11, 1995: With his family at his side and in front of a Monday night crowd, Marino receives congratulations from Tarkenton for his record-breaking accomplishments. On the right is team owner Wayne Huizenga and wife Marti.

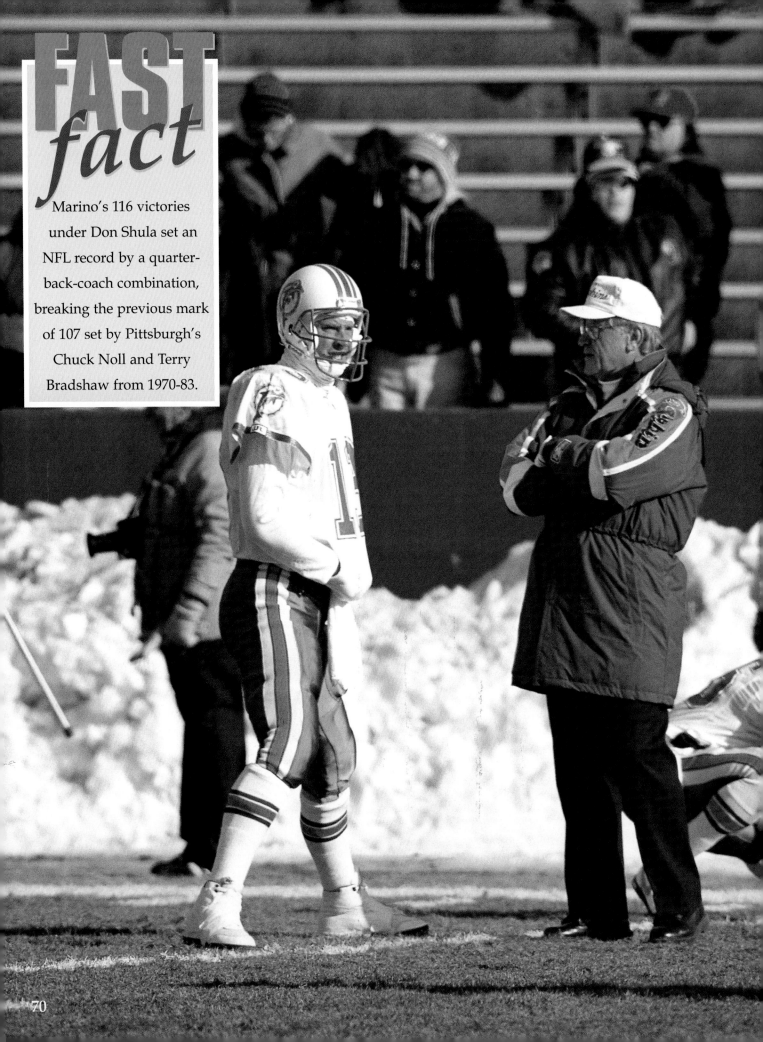

Marino's 116 victories under Don Shula set an NFL record by a quarterback-coach combination, breaking the previous mark of 107 set by Pittsburgh's Chuck Noll and Terry Bradshaw from 1970-83.

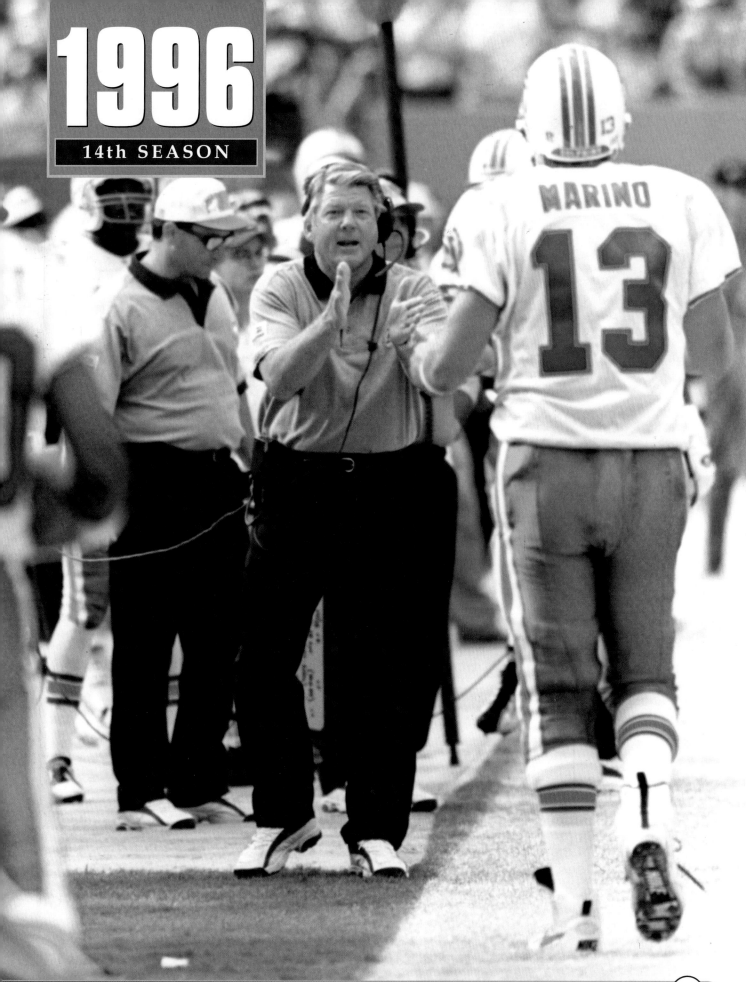

1996
14th SEASON

A new head coach, Jimmy Johnson, would greet Dan Marino and the Dolphins in 1996.

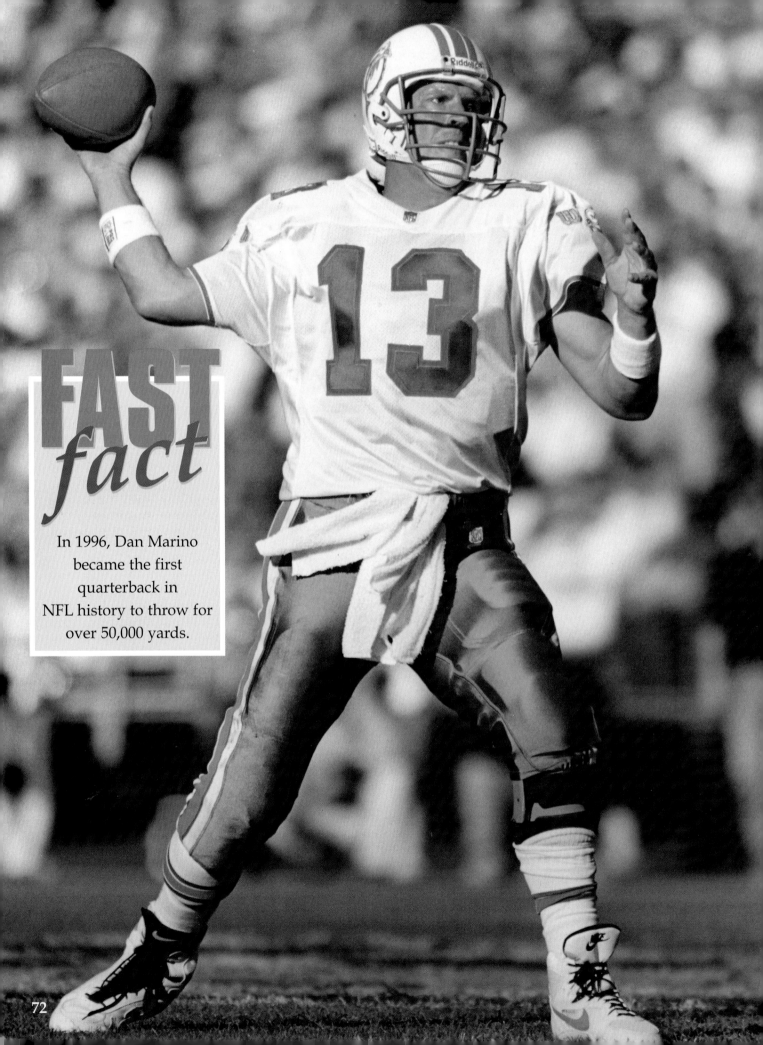

FAST *fact*

In 1996, Dan Marino became the first quarterback in NFL history to throw for over 50,000 yards.

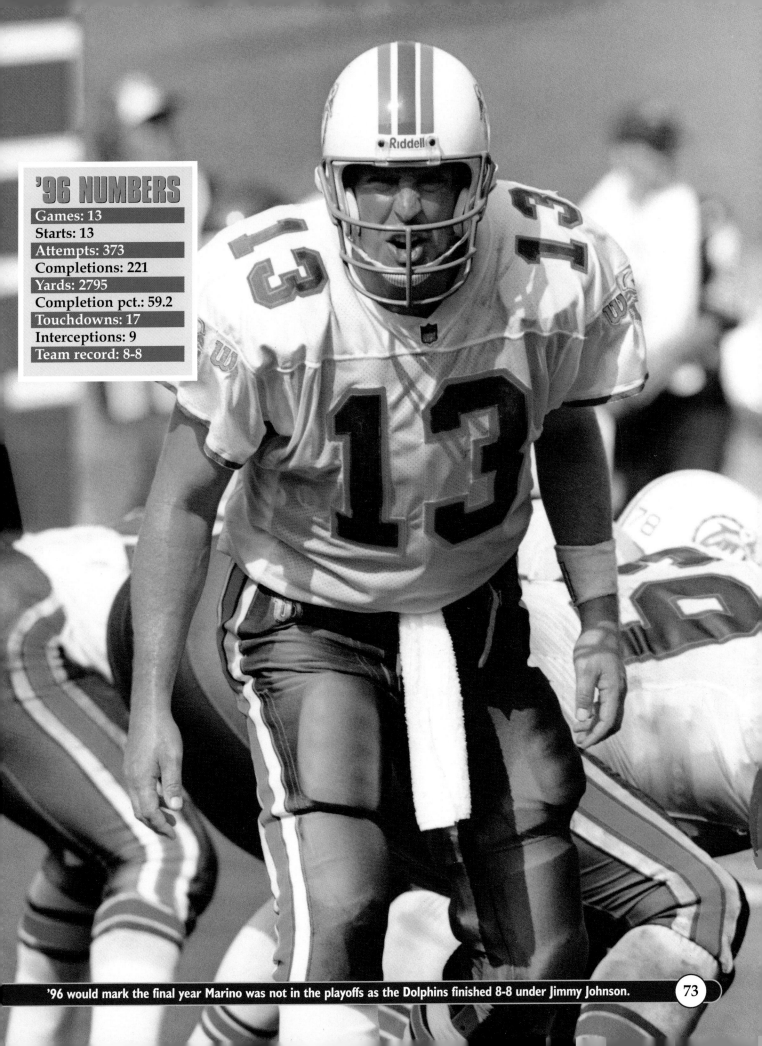

'96 NUMBERS

Games: 13
Starts: 13
Attempts: 373
Completions: 221
Yards: 2795
Completion pct.: 59.2
Touchdowns: 17
Interceptions: 9
Team record: 8-8

'96 would mark the final year Marino was not in the playoffs as the Dolphins finished 8-8 under Jimmy Johnson.

"

Dan Marino amazes me every year. Anybody who thinks he is over the hill is plain wrong. We still need him. We still want him. We still love him.

— **GUARD KEITH SIMS**

Nov. 10, 1996: Marino becomes the first NFL player to record 4,000 career completions with a pass to Fred Barnett against the Colts.

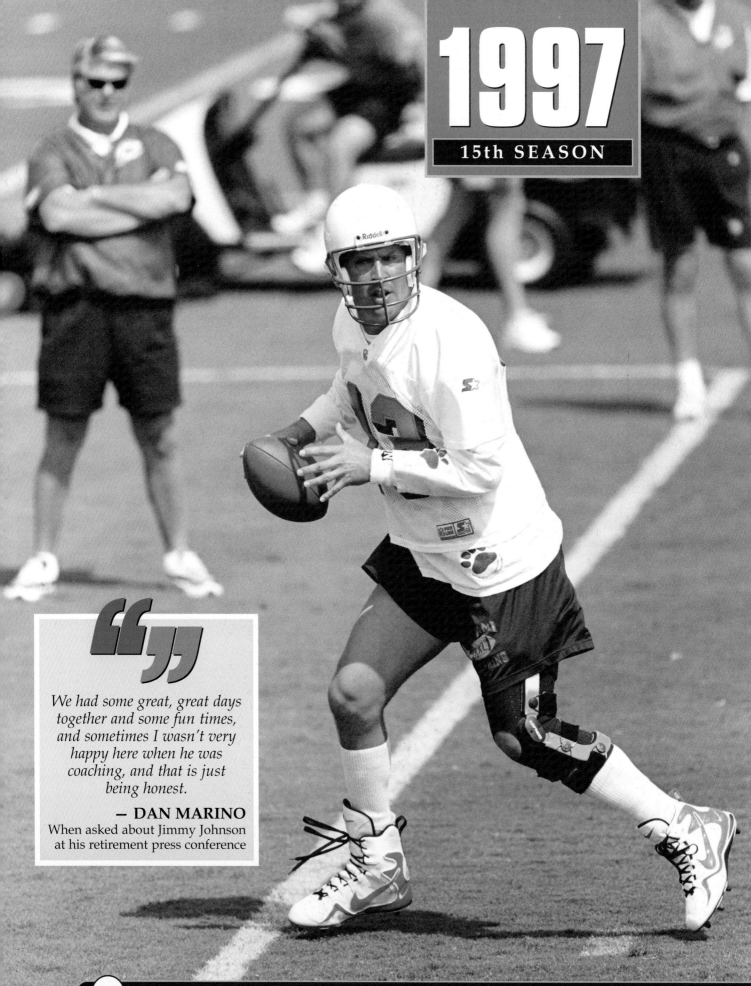

"

We had some great, great days together and some fun times, and sometimes I wasn't very happy here when he was coaching, and that is just being honest.

— DAN MARINO
When asked about Jimmy Johnson at his retirement press conference

Marino, Jimmy Johnson (l.) and the Dolphins came to training camp in 1997 with hopes of a return to the playoffs.

'97 NUMBERS

Games: 16
Starts: 16
Attempts: 548
Completions: 319
Yards: 3780
Completion pct.: 58.2
Touchdowns: 16
Interceptions: 11
Team record: 9-7

Sept. 7, 1997: Marino and the Dolphins were off and running with home victories over Indianapolis and Tennessee (above). 77

> " "
> *He's on fire. When he is, we're pretty much unstoppable.*
> **– WR LAMAR THOMAS**
> After win over Jets

Oct. 12, 1997: Marino is all smiles prior to a 372-yard day and a 31-20 victory over the Jets at the Meadowlands.

Dec. 30, 1997: The Patriots would be the Dolphins' downfall in '97, as they beat Miami three times, including the playoff game at New England.

Nov. 8, 1998: Marino opens the game against the Colts with nine straight completions, and finishes the first half 16 of 19 with two touchdowns, including a 61-yarder to O.J. McDuffie. The Dolphins go on to win, 27-14.

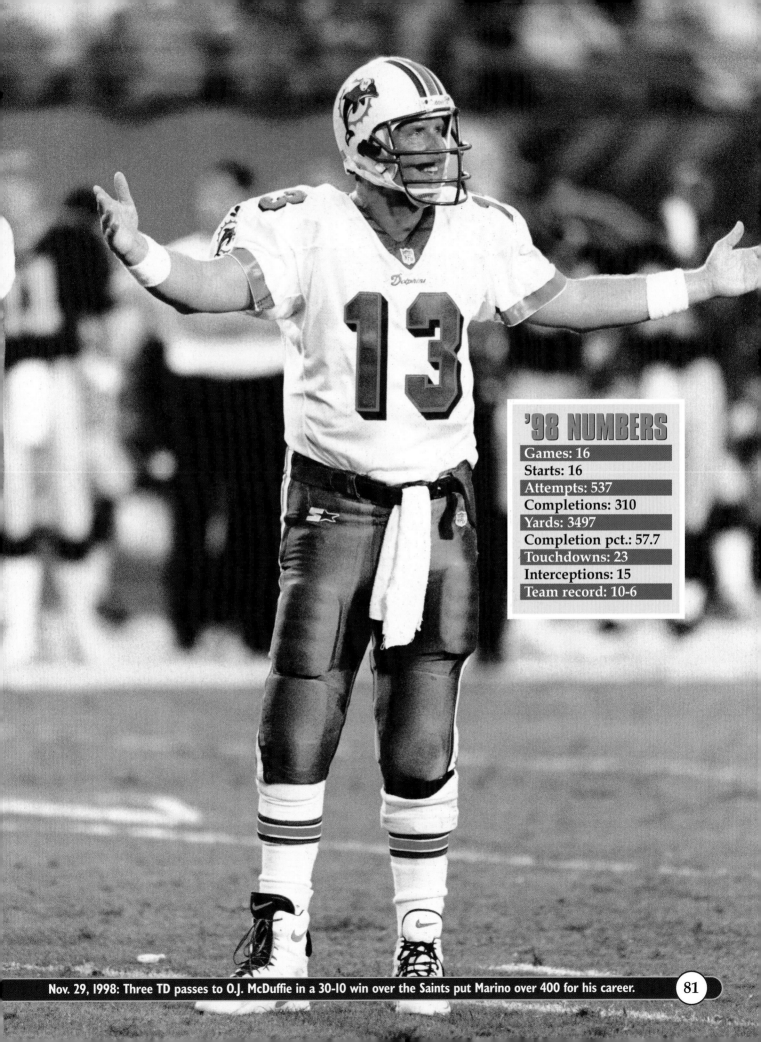

'98 NUMBERS

Games: 16
Starts: 16
Attempts: 537
Completions: 310
Yards: 3497
Completion pct.: 57.7
Touchdowns: 23
Interceptions: 15
Team record: 10-6

Dan Marino didn't win this jump ball off a deflected pass, but the Dolphins did beat the Bills in the wild-card game.

MAN OF THE YEAR

*Jan. 28, 1999:
Dan Marino is named
the 1998 Sprint/NFL
Man of the Year,
recognizing community
service and excellence
on the field.*

The Miami Children's Hospital Dan Marino Center for children with chronic medical needs opened in 1998.

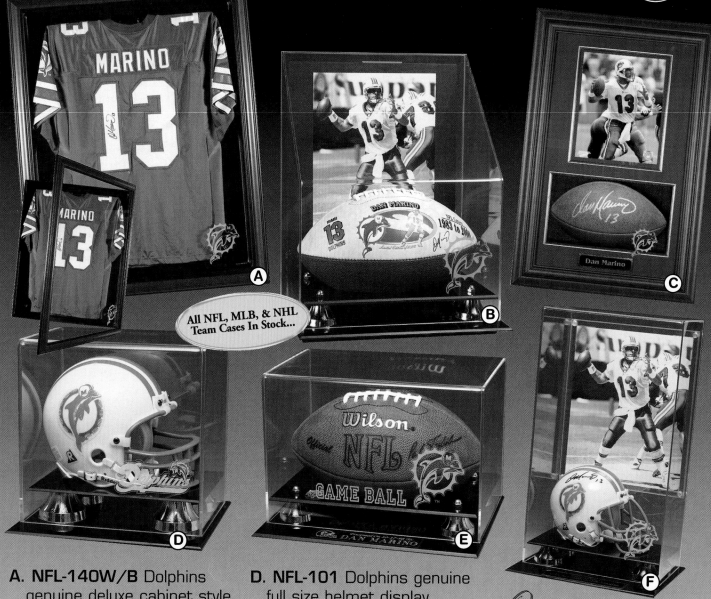

Marino threw more career touchdown passes in the second quarter (155) than in any other. Marino threw 99 TD passes in the fourth quarter, 97 in the third, 68 in the first, and one in overtime.

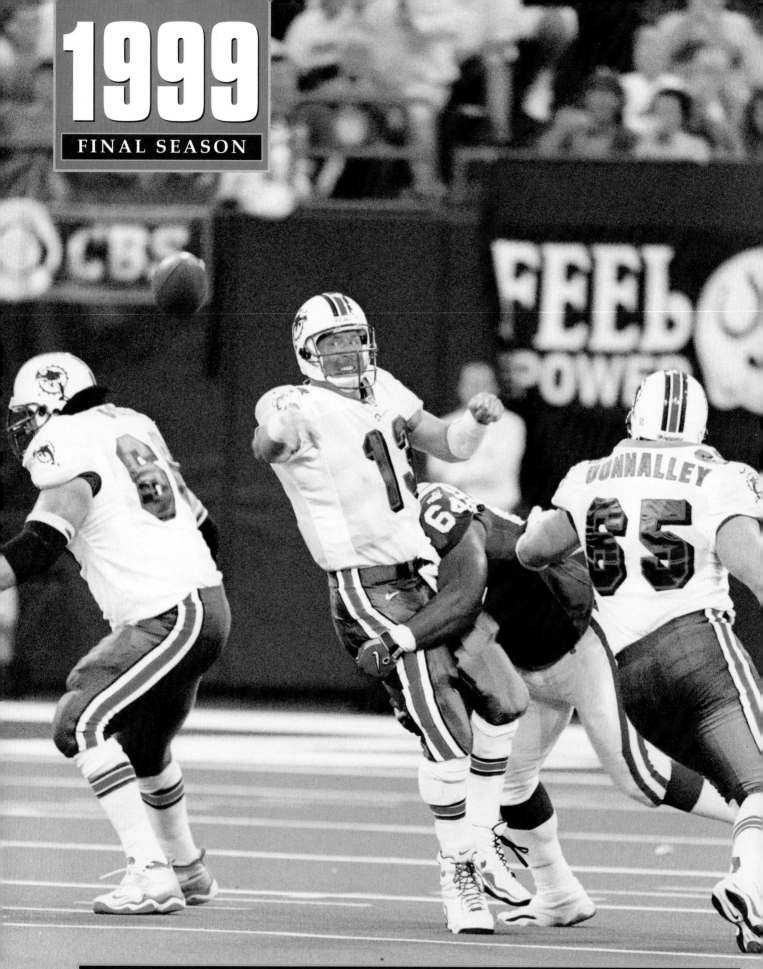

Oct. 10, 1999: Marino throws for 393 yards in a 34-31 win over Indianapolis and is named AFC Offensive Player of the Week. He received the same honor a month earlier after the Dolphins' season-opening 38-21 victory at Denver.

'99 NUMBERS

Games: 11
Starts: 11
Attempts: 369
Completions: 204
Yards: 2448
Completion pct.: 55.3
Touchdowns: 12
Interceptions: 17
Team record: 9-7

You could see it in his eyes on that last drive. He wanted to win so bad.

—WR ORONDE GADSDEN
After playoff win over Seattle

Jan. 9, 2000: Marino orchestrates a vintage fourth-quarter comeback, an 85-yard march through the Seahawks defense in the Dolphins' 20-17 playoff win at Seattle.

During what would be his final fourth-quarter comeback — and his final NFL victory — Marino showed the same intensity he brought to every game of his career.

FINAL GAME

Dan Marino would play his final NFL game on January 15, 2000, a playoff loss at Jacksonville. Coming off the big road win against the Seahawks in the first round, hopes were high for another victory that would get the Dolphins into the AFC Championship game. But it was not to be. The Jaguars dominated the first half, and Marino went in for one final series to start the second half. When Marino came off the field with 13:22 left in the third quarter, it would be for the last time. Everyone in attendance had witnessed the end of a legendary career and, for his many fans, a moment they wished would never come.

> "
>
> *Just to be able to have played with him is something special, because when you think of the Miami Dolphins, you think of Dan Marino.*
>
> **— LB ZACH THOMAS**

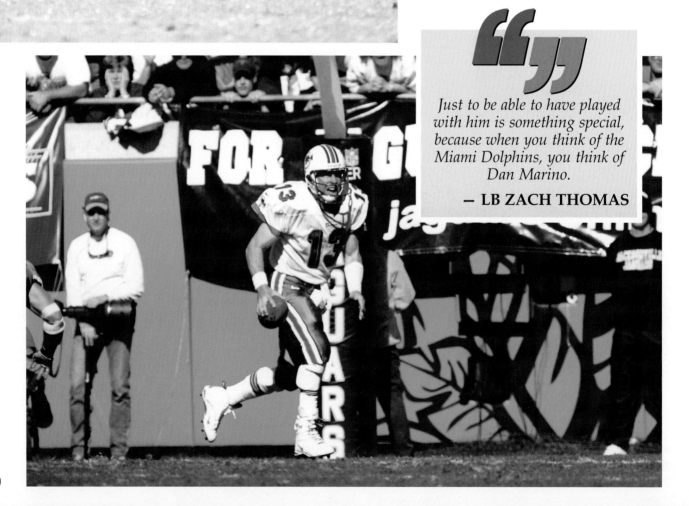

Dan Marino won AFC Offensive Player of the Week honors 18 times, more than anybody else in the league since the award was first given out in 1984.

Marino's final **AFC Offensive Player of the Week** honor came for his efforts against the Colts early in the 1999 season.

RETIREMENT DAY • March 13, 2000

Hello, everybody.

I want to thank you all for coming. After 17 years I would like to announce my retirement from the Miami Dolphins. After playing the game of football for most of my life, this was an extremely difficult decision.

But I know that I have made the right decision for me and my family.

I am very proud of the success that we have had as a team for 17 years, as well as all my individual accomplishments. Not many people have an opportunity to spend 17 years of their life doing what they truly love to do. And as I stand here before you today, I can say that I have been blessed with a career greater than I could have ever imagined.

I am extremely proud of the fact that I was able to play 17 years for the Miami Dolphins. And I am going to miss it. I am going to miss everything about it. I am going to miss the relationships with the players. I am going to miss the fans. I am going to miss the great friends that I have made over this time. I am going to miss all the good times that we have had together. But most of all, I am going to miss Sunday afternoons.

There are not many situations in life that can compare to the emotions, the competition and the preparation that go into a football game. It is a great game.

I have been blessed over the years to have a great family and support from them, and today they are here. My mother and dad are here. I want to thank them for everything over the years, the support that they have given me, and it is special because through my whole career ever since I have been a little boy, they have been able to watch every game that I played. There are not many guys that can say that. To my dad, he is the best coach I have ever had. Thank you, both.

To my wife, Claire, we have been through this 16 years together. We have had a lot of ups and downs, but we have accomplished a lot of things. You have always been by my side. You are an incredible mother and you are my best friend. Thanks.

We have five fabulous children, Michael, Dan, Joey is just smiling — what, Joe, this is not easy, Joe. Ally and Niki, guys, I was always hopeful that I would play long enough for them to see me play the game that I love and they were able to do that and I hope they always have fabulous memories of me being a Miami Dolphin. Thanks, guys.

There are so many people that I would like to thank, starting with the Robbie family. I want to thank the late Joe Robbie and his son, Tim, for giving me the opportunity to play here, and a special thanks to the Huizenga family, Wayne and Marti. You have

always been very supportive and it was an honor to have been a part of your football team, but most importantly I want to thank you for your friendship.

I am honored that Coach Shula is here today. Coach, not only have you been a tremendous impact on my career, but you have taught me how to be a true professional. I am very proud of the fact that we were able to win more games than any other coach/quarterback combination in the history of football.

Thank you to all the coaches that I have worked with over the years and all of the great players.

To the Dolphins staff, the people in the building here that you see each and every day; to our team president, Eddie Jones, thank you; to the guys that work and help the players with what they are doing each and every day; the equipment staff, Tony Egues, Charlie, Joey, guys that are important to the players; a guy that is not here anymore is Bobby Monica, he is a friend. Trainers, guys that take care of me, getting me in shape, try to make me the player that I am, Ryan Vermillion, Troy Maurer, Brad Roll is here and John Gamble, thank you. And the public relations staff, Harvey Greene has been great, 11 years I have worked with Harvey. Fudge Browne, community relations, thank you, Fudge. There is one person that is kind of unique, our video man Dave Hack, he is the only person that has seen every touchdown pass that I have ever thrown. I thought that was kind of neat.

I have played with so many different players over the years and thrown touchdown passes to 51 different players, but there were some special players in my career that I would like to acknowledge. When I started out here with the Miami Dolphins, I had a great group of receivers — Mark Duper, Mark Clayton, Nat Moore, Jim Jensen, Jimmy Cefalo — but there will always be a special place in

my heart for Duper and Clayton. They caught more touchdown passes than anybody that I have ever played with. As they have always said, they made me look good; they made me a star. (laughter).

Don Strock, thanks for helping me when I was a young quarterback. Thanks to Dwight Stephenson, who was the most incredible leader on the field. He is a Hall of Fame player, as well as a Hall of Fame person. Thank you, Dwight, and more recently to Richmond Webb, who was on my left side and took care of me for so many years, and to probably the toughest football player I have played with, O.J. McDuffie.

Thanks to all of you guys, you have made life easy for me. Some special friends that are here — Marvin Demoff, we have been through a lot this past month. I want to thank Marvin for coming from Los Angeles. Another person, Ralph Stringer, who has helped me a lot in my community work here. I want to thank him.

I want to thank the members of the media for covering me throughout my career and supporting a lot of things that I do, charitable-wise. I have some close friends that have done a lot of work with me, and I appreciate that.

Finally, to the Dolphins fans. It has been an honor to play here in front of great and supportive fans. Together we have shared many memories. I feel that I have always had a special relationship with Dolphins fans everywhere. I thank you for being behind me throughout my career. I hope you have enjoyed these 17 years as much as I have.

I want to thank everybody in the organization, all the players I have ever played with, my family and the media coming out here today. It has been great. Thank you very much.

QUOTABLES

"To me, Dan is the greatest competitor among the over 2,000 athletes I have coached. His will and determination are legendary and I've never been around someone who wants to win as much as Dan."

— DON SHULA

◆◆◆

"I can honestly say I played with The Man. He simply was the best that ever played. He left a mark on the game that will never be duplicated."

— MARK CLAYTON
Former Dolphins wide receiver

◆◆◆

"He is the best, not only on the field but off of it, too. I'm honored to say I played against him and something even more special — that he's a true friend."

— JIM KELLY
Former Buffalo quarterback

◆◆◆

"Dan made me look good so many times. … Shoot, he made me! I'm gonna miss him."

— O.J. McDUFFIE
Dolphins wide receiver

◆◆◆

"Dan Marino did all of the things that winners need to do. He did it with class and he had a style about him."

— DWIGHT STEPHENSON
Hall of Fame center

"He was without a doubt one of the greatest passers and toughest competitors in the NFL's 80-year history. Dan combined a fiery will to win with an unmatched ability to take charge at the most critical juncture."

— PAUL TAGLIABUE
NFL Commissioner

◆◆◆

"You have to admire Dan's greatness on the football field. He hated to lose and that speaks volumes to his greatness."

— KEITH JACKSON
Former Dolphins tight end

◆◆◆

"You never really can appreciate something until it's gone. And I think that's what a lot of Dolphins fans and people around the NFL are going to realize. Dan was able to teach people a lot of lessons, not only how to handle yourself on the field, but the way to carry yourself off the field."

— RICHMOND WEBB
Dolphins offensive tackle

DAN MARINO MVP AWARD

At the 1999 Miami Dolphins Awards Banquet, the Dan Marino MVP Award was unveiled by team president Eddie Jones (c.). The award, bearing a statue of Marino setting up to throw, will be given out annually to the Dolphins' most valuable player. Marino himself was voted the team MVP by the South Florida media 12 times.

The first annual Dan Marino MVP Award is presented to defensive back Sam Madison (left) for his play in the 1999 season.

ChildNett
a powerful message
By Dr. Roberto Tuchman

Power is a word with many meanings. In fact power as a word expresses a concept that varies depending on the circumstances. I can recall an incident that occurred to me back in 1992 that helped me understand the meaning of power in a fashion that I had not thought of before. I had been taking care of a child with a neurodevelopmental disorder and had seen him in my office with his mother on two separate occasions. The problem was that the interventions being suggested by other professionals and myself were not being carried out because the father did not agree with our professional opinions. I had never had an opportunity to meet or discuss these issues with the father of this child, as he had not participated in any of our appointments or discussions. At one visit I was surprised to see the father bringing his child in for the medical appointment.

As I introduced myself to him he cut me short and looking at me straight in the eyes said "listen doc, the only reason I'm here is because I heard Dan Marino's son has a problem similar to my son's and if he can ask for help so can I". Over the next few months interventions were begun, the child improved and the father became an active participant in the treatment and success of his son. Dan Marino did not ever see this child, he at least to my knowledge does not even know who they are, yet this incident demonstrated to me that power can transcend not only physical but also professional boundaries. Dan had achieved what I and other health care professionals were not able to do which was the powerful act of facilitating this father's participation in his son's care and as such allowing these interventions to succeed. That is power.

The story gets even better. A couple of years after this incident Dan and Claire Marino had the vision to understand that the power of their name could have a positive impact on the lives of children throughout South Florida. They had the power of vision to help create the Dan Marino Child NETT (Neuro-developmental and Evaluation Treatment Teams) which is the operating arm of the Miami Children's Hospital Dan Marino Center and which opened its doors in March of 1998. In 1999 the Dan Marino Child NETT has coordinated programs that accounted for 25,000 visits to the Dan Marino Center. The power to transform the lives of these children is now a reality and those of us who have the honor to work at the Dan Marino Center take this responsibility very seriously.

The story does not end here. The power of the Dan Marino name can be seen in the almost daily emails we have received from all parts of the world. Over the past year the power of the Dan Marino Child NETT has extended way beyond South Florida and we have had children receiving care at the Dan Marino Center from a variety of regions around the world. This summer we had six families from Italy bring their children for eight weeks to receive interventions at the center and these families became an integral part of the larger Dan Marino Child NETT. At times during the summer of '99 the Dan Marino Center was the "little Italy" of South Florida. These families in turn exerted their power on those of us working at the center and allowed us to understand the common bonds that all of us share. In addition, many of us who work at the Dan Marino Center have also had the opportunity to travel and lecture throughout the United States and to countries in South America, Europe and the Middle East. The power of the Dan Marino Child NETT message has now touched many corners of the world. The message is simple yet powerful: If we work as a team we can have a positive impact on the lives of all children.

Everyday those of us working at the Dan Marino Center experience the power attached to the name of our center and we strive to take advantage of this to transform in a positive fashion the lives of the children and families we encounter. Those of you participating in this golf tournament either as celebrities, volunteers or as guests also have chosen to use your power to add to our message and better the lives of children. All of us working at the Dan Marino Center and the children and families we serve thank you. We will harness this power and the Dan Marino Child NETT will deliver your message to all that care to listen. To be continued.

—*Roberto Tuchman, M.D., is the Executive Medical Director of the Dan Marino Center, Department of Neurology, Miami Children's Hopspital*

April 14, 2000: Marino's locker is encased in glass and becomes a permanent fixture in the Dolphins locker room.

Following the ceremony Dan poses in front of the locker with wife Claire, their children and his parents.

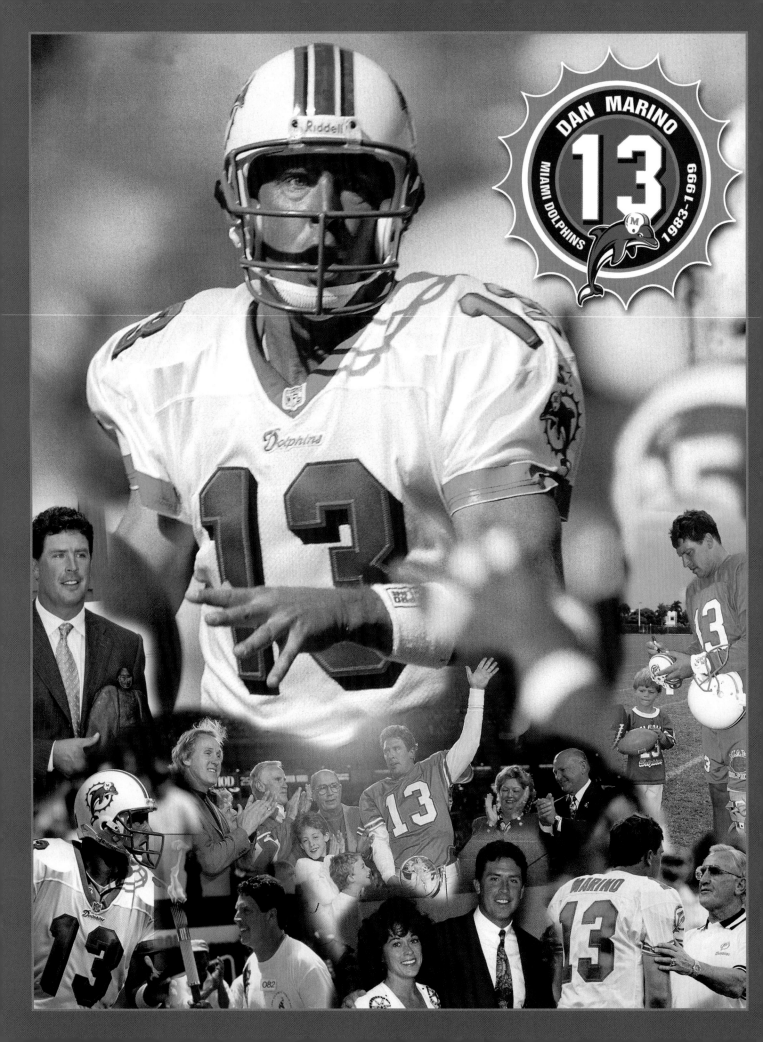

DAN MARINO
13
MIAMI DOLPHINS
1983-1999

THANKS DAN,

FOR 17 YEARS OF GREAT MEMORIES!

Your Friends,

OFF THE FIELD

Dan's success on the field led to many product endorsements, from cars and gloves to sports apparel.

Marino with sportscaster and former Steelers great Terry Bradshaw prior to the Dolphins' 45-28 AFC Championship game win over Pittsburgh on Jan. 6, 1985. Marino threw for 421 yards and four touchdowns in the game.

Dan poses with Joe Montana during a media session in London before the American Bowl on July 31, 1988.

Dan with son Daniel and good friend and former teammate Don Strock after a Nov. 5, 1989 win over the Colts.

Marino helps distribute relief supplies after Hurricane Andrew devastated South Florida in August 1992.

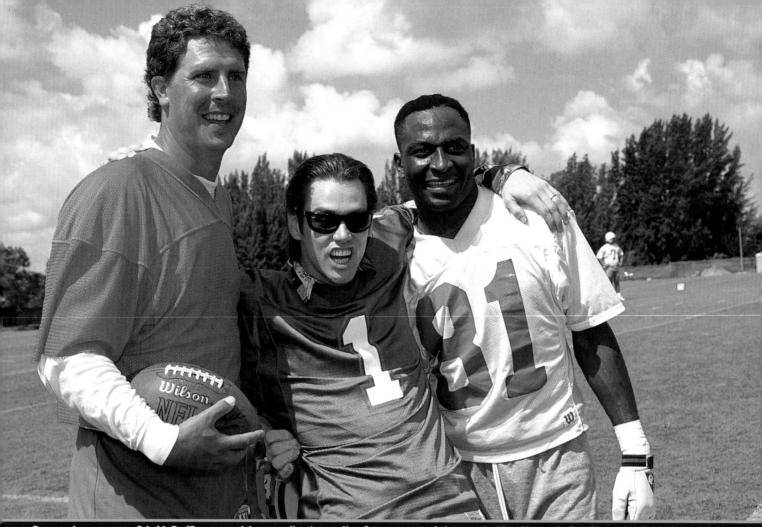

Dan and teammate O.J. McDuffie pose with comedian/actor Jim Carrey, star of the movie "Ace Ventura: Pet Detective." Marino played himself in the 1993 surprise box office hit.

During a break from filming, Marino enjoys some laughs with former Dolphins Dwight Stephenson (back to camera), J.B. Brown, Joe Rose, and star Jim Carrey.

Marino was honored to carry the Olympic torch as it traveled through South Florida on its way to the 1996 Olympics in Atlanta.

Dan and Santa take a break during a photo shoot for Dolphins Christmas cards in 1998.

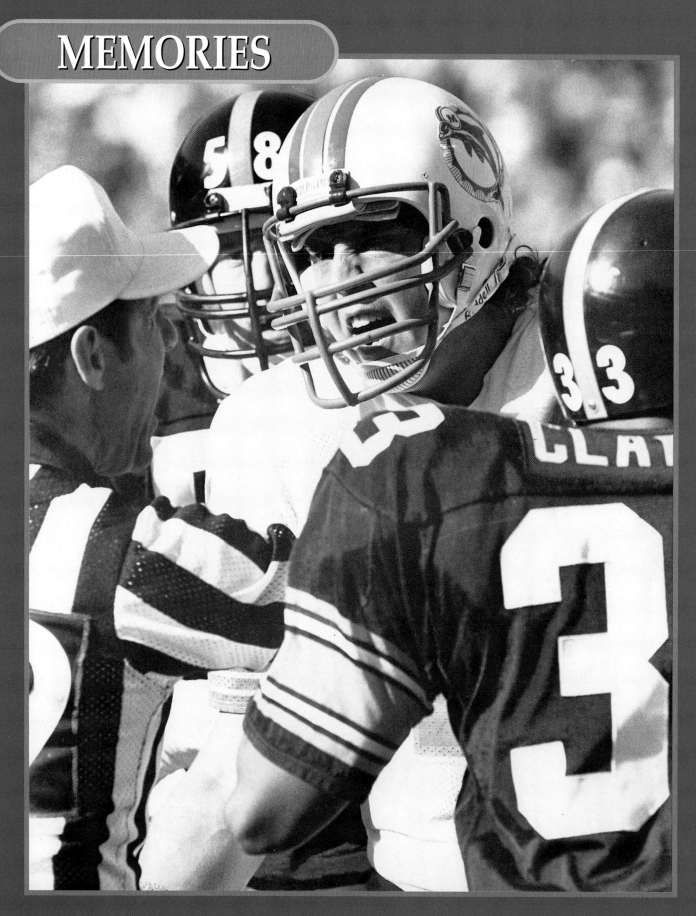

Jan. 6, 1985: Marino is fired up during a discussion with a referee and Pittsburgh's Jack Lambert during the AFC Championship game. Marino burned the Steelers with 421 yards passing and four touchdowns in the 45-28 rout.

Sept. 4, 1994: Marino dives in the mud for a key first down against the Patriots. The opening-day game marked his return from a serious Achilles injury that ended his season in 1993. Throwing for 473 yards and five touchdowns, Marino served notice that he was all the way back.

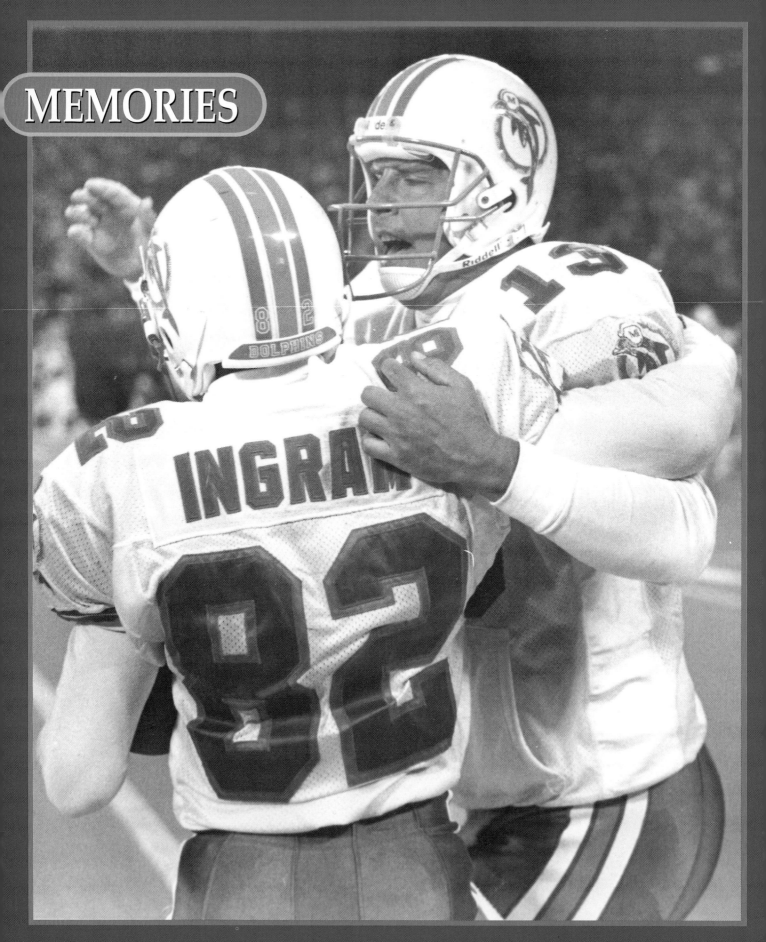

MEMORIES

Nov. 27, 1994: Dan Marino and Mark Ingram celebrate after Marino tricked the Jets by faking a clock-stopping spike, then throwing an 8-yard TD pass to the Dolphins receiver with 22 second left in the game. Marino and Ingram hooked up for four touchdowns in the game, which saw the Dolphins storm back from a 24-6 second-half deficit to win 28-24.

Dec. 21, 1998: Marino outduels John Elway in a highly publicized Monday night battle. The Dolphins win 31-21 as Marino throws for 355 yards and four touchdowns, including three to Lamar Thomas.

MEMORIES

Oct. 10, 1999: Marino and receiver Oronde Gadsden celebrate their game-winning touchdown with 29 seconds to go against the Colts. Marino led the Dolphins to 25 fourth-quarter points, a Dolphins team record.

Marino, alone with his thoughts before the final game of his career, Jan. 15, 2000 at Jacksonville.

PHOTO CREDITS

Ken Keidel/Dolphin Digest
Front cover right, front cover bottom inset. Pages 1, 6, 7, 12, 18, 24, 25T, 26T, 28, 29B, 34B, 35, 38, 41, 42, 43, 45, 47, 48, 56T, 56B, 57B, 58, 64, 66, 70, 73, 79, 80, 81, 85, 86, 87, 91, 106, 107, 108, 109, 110, 111. Back cover.

JC Ridley/Dolphin Digest
Pages 51, 77, 82, 88, 89.

Rhona Wise/Dolphin Digest
Pages 68, 71, 72.

Dave Cross/Miami Dolphins
Front cover top inset. Pages 3, 4, 9, 13, 14, 15, 16, 17, 19, 20, 21, 22, 27, 29T, 30T, 31, 32, 33, 34T, 37, 39, 40, 44, 46T, 49, 50, 52, 53, 54, 57T, 59, 60, 61, 62, 63, 65, 67, 69T, 74, 76, 78, 83, 90, 92, 93, 94, 95, 97, 98, 101, 102, 103, 104, 105T, 112.

Alan Schwartz/Miami Dolphins
Page 10.

Al Messerschmidt
Pages 8, 11, 16R, 105T.

Bob Rosato
Page 55.

T = Top, B = Bottom, L = Left, R = Right